HEAVEN'S PEN

Poetry

HEAVEN WHISPERS & SO I WRITE

~ S. M. Hampton

HEAVEN'S PEN

Poetry

HEAVEN WHISPERS & SO I WRITE

Poet & Writer: S. M. Hampton, Chicago, Illinois

Email: authorSMHampton@gmail.com

Facebook: Heaven's Pen; S. M. Hampton

Twitter: authorSMHampton

Editor: Kimberly Marie Haight, Golden, Colorado

Book Cover: Travis Miles, Seattle, Washington

Printer: FGS/Kelvyn, Broadview, Illinois

HEAVEN'S PEN

Poetry Series:

Book 1 ~ *Heaven Whisper's & So I Write*

ISBN: 978-0-9862078-0-8

Edited by Kimberly Marie Haight, Golden, Colorado

Cover Design by Travis Miles, Seattle, Washington

Printed by FGS/Kelvyn, Broadview, Illinois, USA

Printed Tuesday, November 11, 2014

INSPIRATION ~

First time I saw you "Love"
My heart flew like a "Dove"
Never had a love so real
You're everything I want to feel.
Never am, afraid to die
At the gate, I will sigh
Never had a love so "true"
Embedded in my heart... is only "you."
~ S. M. Hampton

"Let him kiss me with the kisses of his mouth
For your love is more delightful than wine.
Pleasing is the fragrance of your perfumes;
Your name is like perfume pouring out."
~ Solomon's Song of Songs (NIV)

"*...Her eyes in heaven would through the airy region stream so bright, that birds would sing and think it were not night. See how she leans her cheek upon her hand! O that I were a glove upon that hand, that I might touch that cheek!*"
~ *Shakespeare's Romeo & Juliet*

"*To be nobody but yourself in a world which is doing its best day and night to make you like everybody else, means to fight the hardest battle which any human being can fight and never stop fighting.*"
~ *e.e. cummings*

"*Your talents are nourishing others rather than you. You could change this, but you decide not to bother.*"
~ *Unknown*

"*It is only with the heart that one can see rightly; what is essential is invisible to the eye.*"
~ *Antoine de Saint-Exupery*

"*A candle loses nothing by lighting another candle.*"
~ *James Keller*

IN LOVING MEMORY ~

"Mom, you inspired me in many ways...

As a child, you gave me Christian poetry books. These little books brought forth my love of poetry, humanity and of God. I would get lost in the stories, and how the words would play off of one another. I loved the way that I felt while reading them. They were something beautiful to me and became a part of me.

As a woman, your beauty and strength, your courage and gentleness, have been an inspiration through time. I am inspired to be like you. Many times I have needed to talk to you, but I know in my heart and soul… you are there, and have never left my side. I feel you with me.

Oh, and one more thing mom... thank you for inspiring my love for the theater. I absolutely love it!

Well, I hear the music starting to play in the distance, like I'm at the Oscars.... I miss your beautiful face mom.

I love you so much...

Until I see you..."

"Billy, my warm and loving brother. When it came to knowing the other's thoughts and feelings, we just had this 'thing' neither of us could explain.

I am blessed for all the time we shared together, all the laughter and smiles, our motorcycle rides through Kankakee.

You are always in my thoughts and heart, Billy. Whenever I feel down, I hear you trying to make me laugh. And, it works Every Time!

You just always wanted to make me smile, to make me feel safe, loved and cared for. Thank you for that. As you have often said about others, the same applies to you, "You're good people," and an Amazing Soul.

Billy, the night before you passed, do you remember the humongous hawk that we saw? It was so close, we could have touched it, as it flew above our heads. Well, I think he's a messenger.

Since you left this world on to a better place, I now see hawks everywhere, and feel your presence whenever they are near. Is it you that guides me? Or do you and God send them to remind me you are near? Well, I love seeing them. It makes me happy.

Billy, I know you and Mom watch over Matthew and me. I can feel you. Thank you. You are forever in my heart.

You know what... I smile every time I think of you.

I love you so much…
            Until I see you…"

ACKNOWLEDGMENTS ~

My Son, Matthew Ryan Hampton. "Matthew, before you were born, I dreamed of you...I already knew your name. I am blessed each and every day with a truly wonderful son... by just being you.

With an honest heart-of-gold, you have a way of touching everyone you meet (No, not like that! I know what you're thinking, because we share the same sense of humor!)

Each day I am asked about you... The conversation generally doesn't start off with, "How are you?" It usually starts off with, "How is Matthew?" People know where my treasure lies.

I know you love it when they call me, "Matthew's mom." I wouldn't want it any other way. One day, someone said, "I always call you, Matthew's mom, what is your name?" I told them, but added, "I actually like, 'Matthew's Mom!" We just laughed.

I see how kind you are with others, and see how much they appreciate your kindness towards them. That makes me so very proud of you Matthew. Not many moms can say that their son's impress them every day with their kindness and generosity towards others. But I sure can...

Thank you also for not being afraid to show your feelings towards me, even among your friends. You've never seemed embarrassed to hang out with "mom" or tell me you love me in front of others. That has always meant the world to me. You are a good example for others to follow. You truly are a "Gift of God." You live up to the name, Matthew.

You have had to grow-up independently, and I realize life hasn't always been easy for either of us, but you have turned out to be a Remarkable person, child, and Man. You make me a better person just being around you. You teach me daily about love, life, endurance, strength, and courage, as well as, the willingness to push ahead through any of life's obstacles. Lessons I proudly learn all the time from you! I love you Matthew ...

My "Wind Beneath My Wings."
X...O..."

My Muse, Bill Christy. "You have caused
my Heart to Flutter and my Pen to Swirl –
You are a Heavenly Gift of Inspiration."

Special dedications to all those who have touched my heart and made it sing through the years…

"Through the years, there have been loves and losses. We all have them, move forward in hope of becoming a better person. Celebrating and cherishing special times as well.

I especially dedicate this book to those who have caused my heart to flutter and my pen to swirl ~

Many quiet days and evenings, I have sat and reflected upon love, nature, and of God and Angels. With candles lit and a fire blazing in the fireplace, or being still, and listening to nature, words began to flow, as if someone was whispering them to me.

Thoughts, smiles, tenderness, kisses, and holding people near to my heart, make me smile and light up my soul. Thoughts of beyond this life, of once again being with loved ones, and hopefully, to have touched their lives, in the same way they have touched mine.

This book is dedicated to all those I love… have loved, and who have loved me. I cherish every one of you. And to God, who has blessed me with the wondrous gift of life, and my truest gift, my son."

"So the last shall be the first."
Matthew 20:16

"My world and life would be lost,
lonely and without faith, hope and love…
without God's love in my life.

I hear "Heaven's Whisper" and So I
Write. Thank you Father… for the gift of
penning your words to touch hearts and
souls. You truly work through those of us
who 'believe in' and 'listen to' your whisper.

I have learned to not only believe, but
know, because you have shown me my path
and guided me time-and-time again.
Father, I am blessed to live with you in my
life. I am everything with your Love. I pray
that all who touch this book, are blessed with
the loving words that flow from the pages,
and move into their hearts. I pray their
hearts and souls remain open to love and to

all things Beautiful. Touch them Father with Faith, Hope and Love.

Thank you, Father....

Amen. "

INTRODUCTION ~

When was the last time you received a hand-written letter? Remember the love letters you received when you were young? How you felt? Such an innocent expression of how their heart and soul felt. I hope you have these memories.

In high school, my boyfriend knew which friends would be in my classes. Every day, he asked them to give me notes. They were folded like a football. What made it even sweeter, we would see each other between classes and after school…and yet, he still gave love letters to me. I did the same.

We spoke and fantasized about life together. To be married and what our children would be named. It was innocent and beautiful. We were never afraid. We simply expressed our love for one another.

Shortly after high school, he passed away. And yet, he still is with me, and leaves me dimes, and often, in the strangest of places. At times, I smell his cologne, and can feel his arms around me. Protecting me. Caring for me. Perhaps, one day, I may put our love letters in a book. These are memories to treasure.

The losses within my life have taught me to express my love. What if the one you love is gone tomorrow, and you didn't get to tell them how much you love them, and how blessed you have been, and what a better person you are, for having them in your life.

Love is what we long for most in life. Embrace it and express how you feel.

~ To yourself be true…

…live with no regrets ~

ABOUT THE AUTHOR ~

"My name is Susan M. Hampton. I was born and still live in Chicago. I am by profession, in Sales & Marketing, for a printing company. My truest passion however, is being a poet and writer. I graduated from DePaul University, June 2012, with my Bachelor's degree in English Literacy and Writing. My wish is to touch people with poetry inspired by love's and Heaven's Whisper.

With time, I have come to believe the world has lost its innocence and romance. People are seeking old-fashioned romance and true love. And then again, perhaps, that is just what I am seeking. Gentlemen, what happened to romancing a woman with poetry and words of love? Asking for a dance under the moonlight and walking her to her door. Ladies, what about the little notes tucked in his pocket? Or mailing a hand-written letter? When was the last time you read Shakespeare or poetry to your children?

In my heart, I believe that we all want to go back to some of the simpler, and heartfelt moments of life's treasures. Write him a love letter or poem today. Write her a love letter or poem today, and let's begin to Feel and Enjoy Love again. The way we were meant to feel it. Romance each other and allow your heart to speak. It may have been told to keep quiet for too long.

I hope the words penned by me inspire your heart and your soul. God bless each and every one of you."

~ Poems ~

POEMS

Free Spirit Fly

Close your eyes and listen to the songs.
The songs nature orchestrates just for you.
Listen deeper.
Feel every vibration.
Listen with your soul.
When willing, your soul has ears to listen.

Embrace the love and compassion of God,
And of Nature.
As you listen… feel God wrap his arms
Ever-so-gently around you.
Think of those you love.

Reflect on all we teach, and learn, from one
Another.
It is more than we realize.

Embrace the goodness and sweetness, to
Deliver peace into your heart...
And the tenderness, to grace tranquility into
Your mind.

Rest my friend, love, student, my teacher...
We are trees that nestle together.
Strength is given, when the other is in need of
Support.

Storms of life do come... none within the
Embrace will fall to the ground or crumble.
Given a chance to become strong again.

Become one with nature.
With one another.

"The light in me... sees the light in you."

You, yourself are nature.
Play the music of "your" song...
And
Free
"Your" Spirit
That longs...

To

~ Fly ~

My Soul is Alive

Once in a Rare while
Someone comes along
Who takes your Breath Away.

Suddenly…
As if awakened
From a deep sleep.

You see an
Effervescent light within their eyes.
They
Captivate your love,
Rescue you from the darkness of this world,
From the loneliness within.

Drawn into the magical fantasy
Where love lifts you high,
Surrounds you,
Awakens your
Soul.
You are Alive!

Kiss after sweet kiss.
Moment after longed for moment.
Falling deeper into your song,
Of loving grace.

Our souls drawn together.
They sing to one another.

Heaven is felt. . .

. . . You are

My Breath.
The Life within me.
My Rescue in a storm.
The Light I run to.
One who touches me…
Makes my Soul Dance with Joy.
You are…
…. My Love.

Matthew, "Gift of God"

You are my 'Greatest Gift'
And why I named you
Matthew.
Your kindness is
Immeasurable
To all you meet.
I am so proud to call you
Son.

A true blessing from God.
You radiate...
With a love
That shines from your eyes.
With a love that flows
From your heart.
No one

Will ever
Replace you.
You are
A blessing
From Heaven…
An "Angel-sent…"

"Gift of God"

Mother

It's 'Your' beauty
I see in my face,
Honest love
Full of grace.
Never complained
Always a fighter,
Fought to make
My childhood brighter.
You're in my heart
Where I carry you,
Reflections
In these eyes of blue.
I feel blessed
Calling you mother,
One day again . . . we'll see one another.

Brother

When I think of you,
I see your smiling face,
I hear your laughter.

When I miss you,
Your humor
Comforts me.

I'll forever remember the day
You stopped by.
Me, so excited and surprised.
Ran outside, hugged you and cried.

Unsure at the moment why
I held onto you so tight.
I never wanted to let go,

Just hold you forever.
I always felt safe when you,

My brother
Held me tight.
So safe and loved.

It was like
"Our Souls Knew…"

So few days left on Earth together.
Special days to be shared…

Before you passed.

To look upon the 'live' reindeer.
To tell you, "I believe."
To be touched by a hawk, so close, we could
Touch it.

A memory, yet symbolic.

Awed by its majesty, its beauty.
Hawks to lead me and guide me
From that moment on.

I think of you and I miss you.
And love you even more.

I will see you again though
Because, my wonderful brother...

"I believe."

True Friend

You're a true friend
Where do I begin?
Through thick and thin
You've always been there.
Never did I wonder
If I had someone to call,
I knew I had a "True Friend."
I could stomp around in ripped jeans.
Hair in a mess.
Something in my teeth.
You could care less.
Saying goofy things
Didn't faze you at all.
It was your access pass.
You've seen me
Rise and fall,
But you stayed,

Regardless of it all...

You're a True Friend

The Wonder of Us

Crave all before us
When souls are close
Time is an orchestrated symphony.

Heart's pound
Beat in unison
Temperatures rise
Insatiable kisses
Nectar of love.

Silent days
When apart.
Daydreams of last encounter.
Quiet and adrift in thought.
Smiling thoughts of togetherness.
Euphoric with anticipation

Of being together

Wrapped In ~

The Wonder of US

"My Muse"

You

Simple thoughts of moonlit treasures
Can't be bought by any measure.
Sparkling hearts, tingling toes,
Washes away all our woes.
Dancing magically to our beating hearts,
Near or far, never apart.
Holding you in a sacred place,
Where time and distance know no space.
You're tucked safely, deep within my heart,
Knowing you were the one, from the start.
No one else touches me, so it seems,
Because... I carry "you" in my dreams.
Moments like this, I have never felt... ever!
It's clear to me, you will live in my heart...
forever.

Love's Nectar

The sweetest
Nectar
Of love's
Innocent fragrance...
Rushing hearts soar.
Giving life
To the soul's butterfly...
Now free to fly
In splendor,
And all the glory
Of your magical touch.
Being alive
Becomes
Beautiful
With you....

My Muse, My Fire

You are my muse, my fire...
...my truest desire.
There's no other lover, only you.

You run with me,
Sing with me,
You are, "The One..."

There's no other stronger, than you.

You are my muse, my fire...
...my truest desire
No flame can hold a candle to you.

Pebbles tap upon my window-pane,
Blue star light and kisses

Promises given… to be your "Mrs…"

A hand to hold,
An arm to take…
A sparkle within our eyes,
When it's "true" love we make.

A blessing, a hope…
All the world can see,
Running wild with the wind,
Letting be…. "What will be…"

My heart keeps burning.
You are my muse, my fire…
…my truest desire!

Just Wondering

I wonder…
Can you feel my breath,
Warm your skin?

Can you feel my kiss,
Caress your face?

Can you see my eyes,
Sparkle, only for you?

Can you smell my fragrance,
Touch all your senses?

You are my love…
Can you feel me,
Long to love you too?

Does my laughter
Fill your heart with joy?

Can you hear my heart,
Beating only for you?

I was just Wondering
As I sit here dreaming of you.

Where I Belong

Hearts pound
To a celebrated
Rhythm.

Gentle eyes
Pierce my soul
With loving arrows.

Your face
Draws me to you
Where I belong.

Lost in the thought of you...
No other place
I long to be,
Than with you.

A lifelong dream and fantasy…
My Love.

I have Found
With you…

My…
True love
My…
True peace
My…
Gentle soul.

Touch me with your wink.
Kiss me gently,
With you I long to be.
The sun awoke…

It rose and kissed
Your slumbering face.

In that moment shared
The brighter you both glow.

My body floats
In your presence.
You fill my senses.

My body
All of me,
Loves you, my love.

Forever in the Rain

Close your eyes
Feel the rain drops
One-by-one.

Each drop
Gently kisses
Your face.

Taste
The raindrops
On my face and neck.

Each intoxicating drop
Is love's potion
I'm falling in
Slow motion.

Just let go…

Feel my lips
Upon your face,
So beautiful
Everlasting grace.

Your eyes
Full of love, longing
For my touch.

Breathe new life
Into our lips my love,
Kiss me…
…Forever in the Rain.

Tonight

Under the sapphire blue sky,
The world gently falls asleep.
The moons light watches guard over the city.

I miss you more and more my love.
I lay here and dream of you,
Think of you and I… "As one."

Under the glowing moon,
We dance with the shadows
Through the peaceful night.

I love you… even when you are not here.
You are on this journey with me.
You remain in my dreams.
I rescue your heart,

And protect you... I will.

When you are not here,
I kiss your face good morning
And once again... each night.

I think of your face
And smile.
I hold you closer and closer
In my heart.

Feel me... wherever you are.
I am closer than you know,
Only a whisper away.

Tonight...
I miss you.

Tonight, as every night…
I fall deeper in love with you.

We Just Knew

The day we first met.
The mere sound of your voice
Made me long for more of you.

Right from the start
A feeling with no explanation, just...
A knowing, A connection.

So relaxing,
Exciting, yet nervous.
So many wondrous feelings!

You seemed timid, maybe even shy.
So was I ...

. . . . as time drew to say goodbye,
We melted in for a kiss . . . and . . .

. . . We "Just knew . . ."

Feel

My love, do you feel me...
When raindrops gently kiss
Your lovely face?

My love, can you feel my love...
Within our warm embrace?

Hear my name
When the church bells sing
To the Heavens.

Feel my tender touch
Upon your cheek
When the wind blows.

Listen intently
As I sing a loving melody
To your heart strings.

Quiet is my whisper in your ear.
Feel my breath upon your skin,
Feel me as the sun kisses your body.

Can you feel my fingers
Run through your hair
When the gentle wind blows?

I embrace you with love,
I "share" with you...
Soft and caressing
My hands when they touch you.

Deep and Passionate
I kiss your lips
. . . with all my soul.

My soul comes alive
And dances only for you
My love.

My life inside me,
My smile maker,
My one and only you.
I love you
More than words can ever express,
So let me show you...

To be so in Love

To be so in love
When apart… to feel their presence.

To feel alive
So free and elated.

To reach new heights!

To feel a longing for their presence.
Want with all your soul.

Just the thought of them is a blessing.
My life and love truly started
…with "you"
"I am in love with you."

You are Her Everything
(Co-written with Kimberly Haight)

To be a woman's "everything" is as easy as a recipe.

Fill her life with romance, with unlimited and overflowing love.

Add passion daily.

Toss in thoughtful times, simple gestures and warm moments through the day to make her heart sing.

Blend in time. Time to discover likes, loves, what pains her. Learn about the child and woman in her.

Sprinkle in care and tenderness.

Mix well the above with desire.

Gently reach for her heart and her soul and fold in your love.

Stand back and gaze upon the mixture of love you are creating.

Is it complete yet?

Perhaps a bit of strength, security and warmth.

Blend within the arms of love to complete this recipe.

Place all the above ingredients in your heart.

Serves two.

Be Brave

Be brave enough to let go,
Although, your heart may break.
The love shared
Will carry you through the days and
Into the nights.
Memories to comfort and
To embrace.
Always "Remember"…
Be brave…

One Feather at a Time

My soul awakens within the silence.
In every direction, my emotions are pulled.
My name, whispered, from the distance.

Awakened by my Father's whisper.
His words resound deep within my soul.

My heart speaks out in silence,
"Father, please take away my pain.
Heal my aching soul.

Allow others to grant me compassion.
Help me to bring down walls, I have built so
High.
My hands that long to reach out, heal them
From their sorrow.

Please, allow me to feel again.
To one day have my heart touched.
Grant me the life I have always dreamed of.

On bended knee, help silence these cruel
Voices…
Whisper peace and health within these frail
Bones.

Strengthen my Body and Soul that time
Has made weak.
Breathe life back into my soul, oh Lord.

I am ready to fly.
You have given me wings…
One feather at a time.
… Amen"

There is Something Special about This One

There is something special about this one.
Warmth is the feeling you deliver.

Joy fills my heart when you speak.
Gentleness fills my soul when you look into
My eyes.

Love and protection fills my life when you
Hold me.

Ever-so-gently, you hold me in the palm of
Your hand.

A precious gem that you treasure.

Sweetly you gaze upon me.
Gentle eyes twinkle, your lips smile
Setting my heart aglow.

Beautiful and loved
How you make me feel…
Touching the depths of me…
There is something special about this one.

Heaven surrounds me.
Gentle, is your touch upon my skin…
…your words upon my heart.

Kisses overflowing with Heaven's potion
Intoxicate me…
Passionately touch my soul.
There is something special about this one.

With your sweet ways.
You show me…
With your words and actions
What love is…
There is something special about this one.

Let us be friends
To talk with.
A smile to count on.
A hand to hold.
To laugh with, to cry with.

Let us be friends
Who not only listen, but truly hear…

Walks in the fresh fallen snow.
Snow angels and sleigh rides…

Walks on the beach.
Holding hands…
Gazing at sunrises – as they fade into sunsets.

To wake in each other's arms,
To kisses and smiles…
A peaceful face, as the moon light shines
Upon it.

To be touched by a Kiss…

Allow us to live and love…
… That possible dream.
There is something special about this one.

Lord, angels high above, please…protect us
Because, "There is something special about
this one…"

True Carino

With the dawning of a new Summer's day
In Stratford-upon-Avon.

The dark room instills peacefulness,
Lit only by the breaking of the brilliant
Morning sun.

He slips ever-so-gently, quietly into her
Room,
Through her trellis-window.

Gloriously she was, as she lay there sleeping.
The warm breeze blew, the linen curtains
Danced all around the canopy bed.

He tenderly moves next to her, affectionately
Gazing upon her,
Touching her cheeks, caressing her hair from
Her face.

Love fills his resplendent heart.
She is his "True Carino" - his Treasure.

The sun shines brightly upon them.
She awakens, finding him next to her.
Love fills her overwhelmed heart.

She touches his cheek and caresses his hair,
His face.
Each captures the other with soul-filled
Longing, admiration and love.

Beautiful her face, lit by the morning sun,
His "True Carino" - his Treasure.

My Sweet Dove

In the middle of the night
I heard
Sweet sounds of a dove.
Fluttering feathers
Wings of an angel.
Sounds of a "dove's" whisper.

His call.
His song found me in a dream.
When I awoke,
I was listening to . . .
. . . My heart, My soul.

His Eyes Fixed on Hers

His heart spoke to hers
From across the room.
As though they met before.
Eyes fixated
On one another.
He slowly glided towards her,
As only a gentleman would.

She takes a step too.
Closer they melted towards one another.
They floated deeper still.
Her attention magnified
With each gentle step.
Hearts raced with fire.
Drawn together by their past.

Precious Pearl

You walk through life with a heart
So bright and golden,
And carry a love, more precious than pearls.

At times, people have crushed your bright
Heart,
And stolen your pearls
Soon after you had let them in the door.

…take my hand,
…let me carry you
To a place that is far from pain,
…where true love resides.

Here you will find peace,
Deep inside my heart…
I will wait for you… there.

Does the Love Still Exist

At the end of the tunnel is a junction – a "Y"
in the road.
Now the decision of which one to choose.
Gingerly walking…
Contemplating desires, wishes and reality.

With a broken heart, walking through the
tunnel. To feel so much love…
With only the heartfelt questions, "Does the
love still exist? … and Am I still loved?"

To only long for love returned, love shared.
Love should not fear love.
Broken hearts do not see the love before
them, even when longed for.

"Do I hold this hand or let it go?"
No one person can keep the flame alive.
Both must burn together.

No more to cry beneath a smile...
Broken hearts may one day heal
...and merge as one.

Let Freedom Ring

Stop, rest and gaze around you...
Look to the skies and see the dazzling stars ~
The puffs of clouds draw pictures for you ~
The mysterious moon writes your story ~
A brilliant sun kisses your face.

Ride along the country-side ~
Breathe it "all" in.
The fresh air through the trees,
Wind blows in your hair.
Fragrant flowers
Caress all of your senses.

Take a barefoot walk on the dewy grass,
Put your toes in the sand.
Walk hand-in-hand.

Pick wild flowers for your lover.
Embrace the natural beauty of it all...

Lost in "its" wonder...
Birds in flight,
Squirrels jumping, playing,
And deer gracing us with their presence.

A child's belly Laugh ~
Remembering, how it is to Play.
Take your lover's hands, and spin ~
Remembering, what it is to "Live..."
This is Freedom ... Let it Ring.

Desire

Thank you for allowing my heart
To "Feel" and "Desire"
Such love again.

To be ready
For new beginnings, new journeys,
. . . and
To see that the path is
Filled with an everlasting light.
Illuminated and filled with love,
Care, nurturing, fun and respect.

To feel protected in your arms,
And in your love for me.

A feeling I have long desired...

Fill my life
With all your amazing love
Within your heart.

Rise Above...
What the world believes love to be,
And remain with me,
By my side.

Mesmerized

Sun light blesses the room
As they enter.
They pause to give thanks to the light.
Peace abounds within their spirit.
Quiet surrounds them.
"Nature pauses..."
Silence touches their lips.
Words are spoken in silence.
Everlasting kiss
From Heaven.
No words spoken ~
Hearts pound as one,
Touching their core.
Mesmerized.

There is Something about Us

There is something about us.
Something, not to be explained.
Even I cannot understand it at times.
Truly... It is beautiful.
A feeling longed for... by lonely hearts
Everywhere.
No mere words to others
Would allow them to understand, how two
Hearts
So far apart,
Are one... and so close.
It is far beyond ... and "Deeper" than
"Us."

Stay

Stay...
Your eyes
Play a song
To my heart.

You strum me
So beautifully...
So gently.

Your voice
Brings peace
Deep inside.

Your touch
Lights a fire
In my soul.

Your Breath
Breathes life
Into this woman.

Stay . . .

It Speaks

Have you ever watched a movie and
Longed for what that couple has?

Have you ever watched young "innocent"
love?
So pure, without fret, jealously or worry?
Before you…you see the Fun and
Freedom.
Run with one another…

"The world is your oyster."

To share that, "Knowing again…"
That, "I'm so much in love with you…"

Suddenly to Feel Alive.

Feelings before me…
Where have you been?

To feel alive again.

Such a joyous emotion flowing within me…

My senses magically awakened,
Healed with life and love's fruitfulness.

The sun shines more brightly on my face.
Joy that
Rises from deep within me...

It speaks…… "Your" name.

There's Only You

Your look into my eyes,
Poetry
Your touch upon my skin,
Electric
Your lips upon my mine,
Ethereal

Your kisses of wine
Make Heaven's light shine.

For me...
"There's only you."

Barren Season of My Soul

It was the brisk, wintery, barren season of my soul. The wind burned my skin with a ruthless slap. Leaves void on the tree of my tender heart. The world bore witness to all my frail, weak branches. With every turn of life, another opportunity snapped another limb.

With each and every breeze, existence seemed to break me a bit more than before.

And yet, unknown to all around me, lying deep below the surface, were strong roots. A life force, filled with great power and strength. Enough to withstand all and stand strong. A great and powerful foundation.

Within this strength and foundation was courage, and the wisdom to know, that one day, the season will change... the sun will emerge, new life will bud upon these barren branches. One day to flourish and grow, taller and more beautiful. As will the season change, and the wind sing a symphony within my growing and budding soul.

Guardian Angel

In the deep, darkness of the night,
Alone and afraid in my room…
The moon gently casts a glow
Through my window.
I know in my soul,
You stand within the glow,
Watching over me.

Only You

I am alone and lost within my senses,
In a room full of people.
He slowly moves towards me.
With eyes closed, I feel your presence.
With each step closer, the more intense my
Feelings grow.
My chest pounds with every heart's beat.
You are near me.
As you stop and caress my hair,
My face...
And still, my eyes are closed...
You've intoxicated my being,
Lowered your face and caressed my lips,
Now, I've melted into your sweet kiss.

I Will Sigh

First time I saw you "Love"
My heart flew like a "Dove"
Never had a love so real
You're everything I want to feel.

Never am, afraid to die
At the gate, I will sigh
Never had a love so "true"
Embedded in my heart... is only "you."

My Once in a Rare While You

Every once in a rare while,
Someone comes along who takes your breath
Away.
Your heart beats faster and faster.
The tingling from the depths of your
Heart…
Meets your toes.
Life is now more vibrant and colorful.
You feel your purpose rise.
Once in a rare while,
You kiss someone who transports you to
Heaven.
My once in a rare while…
….You.

You Know You Have Been Blessed With Love

"Each time you gazed upon the glowing
Moon
The dazzling stars, danced within your eyes
. . . You've thought of him."

Realizing now, you have been blessed with
That "One" love.

Each rising sun's "good morning" light…
Caresses and touches your face.

As it rests for the evening, its beautiful sunset,
Paint's your Love's Story…
And always…
You think of him.

You know you've been blessed with
Something beautiful… "*You know you have*
Been blessed with love… "

Meant to Be

No matter what road life takes me down.
No matter what visions my eyes see.
No matter the flowers that I smell.
The lakes that I gaze upon.
The hurdles that I jump.
Or the people that I meet along the way,
The road always leads me back to you.

Medicine to My Soul

Your voice…
Is Medicine to my Soul.

Your kiss…
Makes my head spin.

The feeling of your skin on mine …
Gives me goose-bumps.

The thought of making love to you,
Sends me to Heaven.

To live without you…
Would leave me lonely, in a crowded room.

Your face, gazing at me…
….is Medicine to my soul.

You my love,
Are Medicine to my Soul.

You are, "The One"

Your laughter,
Is the air that I Breathe.

Your smile,
Quenches my thirst for life.

Your gentle soul,
Sustains
And exalts my life.

You are,
"The One."

My Heart Soared

My heart soared with
Your afternoon call...
Our day we shared, just we two.

My heart soared with
The flowers at the door...
Our dance in the middle of the street!

My heart soared with
The love note...
Followed by our public kiss.

My heart soared with
Your tender touch...
And Gentleman ways.

My heart soared with
The way you...
Make me feel.... Beautiful.

Let's Love Like
We've Never Been Hurt

Your face lights up
As you drive up
And tell me, "Get in."

Music's playing loud,
Singing to our favorite songs.
Wind is blowing through our hair.
The smell of honeysuckle filling our senses.
Laughing 'til we can't breathe.
Stopping at our favorite spot for ice cream
You tap your cone on my nose and
I put mine in your face.

Shyly... you look at me
As if it was our first kiss...
Our eyes twinkle.

Let's love like we've never been hurt.

A Life That Is Golden

I wander around in the world,
And just ponder sometimes...
As the days go by,
I look out the window,
The window of my soul...
At the faces
I see most every day.
I wonder if they're okay.

The old men and
Women walking
The streets,
Begging for a quarter.

Children playing
In the courtyard.
I wonder how it will be
When they get home.

Each night
I pray that God
Touches every
Sheep in his herd.

"Bring them peace, oh Lord," I pray.
"Bring them life,
Prosperity,
Duty.
But more than all of these,
Bring them Love.

A hand to hold.
A friend to talk with.
A love to grow old with.

Bring them blessings and smiles,
Belly laughs and good-company.
Bring them a peace that surpasses
All understanding.

Give them their life changer.
A peacemaker, one who loves
And makes a difference.
And may you bring them
A life that is golden.
     . . . in your name, amen."

Moments to Remember

Tropical winds blew
Through his dark, thick hair.
He gazed out
Into the sunset
Standing in wonder.

He breathed deep
The fragrance
Of summer flowers.
His senses filled
With honeysuckle
Tropical sweetness and
Warm salt air.

Life here was free
And it was perfect…

... The dawn broke

As he walked on the beach,
Watched the seagulls.
And listened to them sing.

All moments created are...
... "Moments to Remember."

His Favorite Songs

Amidst the sweetness...

With a single kiss
The snow sparkles
Beneath the sun's light.

I walk
Thinking of you.
Rainbows dance
On the snow covered plains.

I look up
To see you
Walk towards me.

In slow motion, so it seems

Smiling... I'm gleaming.

My heart races.
I run to you.
Jump into your awaiting arms.

Spun through the air,
... And spun some more!
Falling to the ground.
Laughing, laughing ...
Rolling around...
Slower and slower...
We fall into one another.

Kissing...

You say sweetly,

"The moment I looked upon you...
You must have fallen from grace.
How did you get here?

Where are you from
My Heavenly lady?"

And even softer added,

"Only run to me, never
Away from me.
Hold me forever,
Caress me always...
And be mine...
Til now and til ever!"

Amid the Summer's Day

It was a Summer's Day.
His fingers gently ran
Through her
Long blonde hair.
The taste of sweet honey
Between their lips.

Music and love
Was the theme of the day.
Together they lay
On the sun-warmed beach.
Birds flying and singing.
Sun shining.

The rain began
To sprinkle down ever-so-gently...
The day turned into night.

Now...by the fireside

On the quiet sandy beach,
We are alone.
Under the stars,
Hands entwined.
Smiling and
Spellbound,
By the Beautiful Day...

Today We Say, "I Do"

To love and be loved
Is the greatest gift in life.
To see "that" face,
A heart glows like a sunrise.
To know that their heart
Is thinking only of you.
Longing to see
Your lips kissing theirs.
You my love
Are a mystery to me.
Crazy…Wondering
What I mean to you.
Longing …For your love
And looking forward
To our next moments.

Stay in this Moment

Remembering "first" memories...
That first glance,
Look, in one another's eyes...
Melting...Souls touching
Smiling... just because.
Life together
Love so Heavenly...

Remembering...
The first time touched.
Hands holding
"That" first kiss.
Those lips
Hearts touching...
Love's longing
Remembering...

Sweet memories of moments.
Dreaming of the other
Singing
Dancing
Hearts belonging
Cherishing…

Remembering…
The gift
Cherished together
Recognized
Appreciated
Surrendered to
Loved intensely
Loved passionately
Loved transparently
Loved completely.

Remembering to
Stay in this moment
. . . It is yours.

Live

When feeling alone,
In a world full of people
Meditate and feel present.
Even when you would rather be alone,
Enjoy your own company.

When things are too big
And out of reach,
Remember:
"Climbing is not about
Conquering the rock.
It is about conquering yourself."

When everyone is smiling
And laughing, but you,
Put on your favorite comedy,

Laughter can cure.

When lovers walk hand-in-hand,
And there is no hand to hold.
Hold your own.

When you wish for true love,
And wonder where they are,
They are there, gazing at the same amazing
stars.
You just haven't met them yet.

Live Until Forever

Remembering the first time I saw your face,
So nervous and shy
Like a child.
So bashful, as I leaned into your shoulder.

There you were
So handsome and strong,
Your smile lit up the room and my heart.

I knew from "that" moment,
You were the one for me.

It was a brand new day indeed.

Instantly, my life changed, forever.
So alive and happy.

We laugh and we cry,
We love and we argue.

But we are there for each other,
Just as we want to be.

Thank you for your hand
For your arms around me
. . . And for your kiss.

Thank you for loving my family
Like your own.
Being a leader and a husband.
For showing me... what love is,
And... what love is not.
Thank you for being my friend.
You listened and helped me along the way.

Thank you for allowing me... to be me.
You have shown me incredible strength
...And amazing courage.

I will remain forever changed,
Because... you lived.

For now, I will love "Until" our forever...
... Until then my love.

You Found Me in the Darkness

Through the dark, cloudy night
Your eyes stared intently,
Deeply…
As if you knew me.
My face flushed.
Breath shortened.
Afraid, yet taken by the moment.

That moment, life began.
Feelings never explored,
Not yet known.

My heart began singing,
Yours followed along.

Ours was to be the most beautiful
Song ever heard.
Our souls soared.

Together in flight
We could fly anywhere,
On shared wings, through the night.

Two souls touch as one.

From the Darkness
. . . . Came love's "Life."

Mirror Reflection

I have never seen
The glow that surrounds me.
I have never seen
The smile that adorns my face.

Who is this person
...Before me?
The person
I see
With my reflection
In his eyes.

Awaken My Slumbering Soul

Your gentle touch,
Awakens
My slumbering soul.

Your kiss,
Melts
Away all of my fears.

Your whisper,
Is poetry
Brought to life.

You're My Dream

Eyes
… That put me in a trance.
Eyes
…That capture my thoughts.
Eyes
… That draw me in,
And make me their own.
Eyes
… That make life a dream.
Eyes
… That I dream of.
The sweetest dreams
… Of only you,
My love…
… My dream.

And So My Heart Sings

...And so my heart sings
As the rain slowly falls,
Gently dancing
Upon my face.

Closing my eyes
To feel
Your love
Within my soul.

...And so my heart sings.

My First Dance With You

The night beckons,
Around the
Corner… he steps.
Strong, confident,
Refined and alluring.
I feel faint…
Excitement runs through my blood.
He moves towards me
For passion.
What delicious
Moments…
We will taste, together.
My first dance with you.

Without You

Without you...
My heart is lonely.
Without you...
The sun won't shine.
Without you...
Each day waits...
....for your kiss.

Thinking of You

There is a smile
Upon my face
Whilst I think of you.
Thoughts of you dance
Forever
Through my mind.

A Wife's Love

Grace…Is the presence
She represents.

Peace…Is the gift
Of her heart.

Love…Is what she gives
Forever to me.

Compassion…Is what she draws
Every breath from.

Special…Her care,
Warmth and love.

"She wrote the book."

My Husband

"Oh Lord,

Bring me my desire,

Peace within the storm.

The awe that captures me...

With "His" every word."

Your Smile Warms Me

In the darkness, of my room...

"I feel the warmth
Of your body."

In the darkness, of my room...

"I feel your gentle hands
Run through my hair."

In the darkness, of my room...

"I feel your kiss
Upon my face...
      ...With your Smile."

Shooting Stars, Dancing at Midnight

One summer's eve
We walked down a country road.
Where shooting stars
...Danced upon the Midnight Sky.
Oceans waves sound
Like Heaven's welcoming tunes.

We stood holding hands,
You gazing at me.
Just "we" two...
In our own wondrous world.
Funny it seemed,
Even in a crowd,
No-one was ever around.

Making a wish on those
Shooting stars...
...Dancing at Midnight.

God Will Open a Window

Sitting on the train,
Gazing out the window.
The window of my soul.
I cry out to my Father... In silence.

"I feel so lost and lonely, Lord.
Please, bring me my 'True love.'
Where is "The One" that will love all of
me?"

Suddenly, life stopped.
I felt a Heavenly presence.
Looking upon me.

Silently, we spoke...

It was as if…. 'He knew, all of me…
Every inch…'

I realized…

… He was sent,
Just for me…
…God heard my cry for love.

I Truly Felt Love

At the door was unexplainable peace,
"Peace that surpasses all understanding."

As I open the door,
My life became a whirl-wind
Into Heavenly realms
... To be forever changed.

My Heart, my Soul were on Fire!
Such Intense, amazing feelings of Joy and
Peace.

I truly felt... "Love..."

God loves ALL of me.

Wings of an Angel

In the middle of the night . . . .
                              I heard a dove.

The sound of love.

Fluttering feathers
Wings of an angel
Song playing when I awoke ~

"Baby I'm amazed. . ."

Our Romance

I stick notes in your pocket
For you to find when you want to escape for
A moment.
I think about you...
I feel your energy flow through me.
The passion
When I hug you...
Kiss you...
Make love with you...
...I "Feel" you.

My Addiction

You're like an...
...Enchanting walk in the park,
A swim in the ocean.
You're like the...
Sun upon my face,
The stars in the sky.
You're like a...
Bird taking flight,
A breath of Mountain Air.
You're like a
.... Rush.

~ My Spellbound Lover ~

A lover...
Oh, the sweet embrace
To melt as one.
Peace, Security ... Electricity!
Romance captivates the air.
Enter a room...
Sparkling "Fairy dust"
A magical presence
Illuminates.
Melt into one another...
Slow and gentle
Step by step,
True emotions...
Magic,
Lover does possess.
Closer and closer,

Eyes do capture my heart.
Weaker and weaker with desire,
Lost in the spell.
Faster and deeper to fall...
To feel this spell-binding embrace
Over and over
Again and again.
Drawn close and closer,
Feel light and lighter,
Fall deep and deeper,
Into love...
Weak with feelings,
Kiss of true love desire.
That One lover.
Love with passion,
Love with intent,
Love deeper and deeper,
With sweet ecstasy.

Beyond senses,
Deep intense joy,
Never to feel self-control.
Into sweet Rapture
Lover...
My Spellbound Lover.

~ My Lord, My Mystery ~

Tonight there is a mystery
Sweeping across our great earth.
Something truly special about tonight. . .
A mystery moves through the air.

God's presence abounds and is glorious.
The sky's deep sapphire, with a dusting of
Gems,
Seems to be standing still.
A crisp cool fills the midnight sky.

The north-star stands at attention,
Awaits the presence of our Lord.
People lay in their bed, contemplating
Beliefs.
Thoughts of their daily life

...And the ever "after..."

Praises to you My Lord,
My Mystery ...

HEAVEN'S PEN
Poetry

SOUL SPEAK

Coming Summer 2015